Basic Bible 101

The New Testament Student Workbook
By Margie Smith

This workbook is designed to be used along with *Basic Bible 101*
The New Testament Leader's Guide, or with the podcast of Basic Bible 101
presented by Margie Smith. Reference materials, group leader assistance and answers
to the questions posed here are available on line at www.basicbible101.com. Additional
information about the author, ordering more workbooks, and accessing the student area
of the website can be found on the last page of this workbook. Thank you for purchasing
Basic Bible 101 - The New Testament Student Workbook.

All scripture quotations, unless otherwise indicated, are taken from The New International Version of the Bible.

Basic Bible 101 - The New Testament
Table of Contents

Lesson 1 - What is Basic Bible 101?

Basic Bible 101 is...

1. Basic Bible 101 is a brief overview of the entire Bible, not an in-depth verse-by-verse study

2. Basic Bible 101 is a one year commitment to read the assigned Bible passages, answer the discussion questions, attend every session, study for the quizzes and take the final exam. You may choose to tackle the larger goal of reading the Bible completely through by following the course outline of recommended readings for each week.

3. An opportunity to:
   • Make friends
   • Share struggles and ask for prayer
   • Learn how to apply the Bible to your present situation
   • Strengthen family relationships

What can you expect each week?

In this workbook you will find all your study materials. Additionally we will be using a common version of the Bible, *NIV Student Bible (Zondervan Publishing Co)*, primarily so we will be reading the same words. Throughout the class we will be using the charts and maps included here, as well as other reference materials.

We will begin each week with a review of the previous lesson, then move into a short description of the main story for that day. Your discussion leader will ask some general discussion questions as you work through the Bible passage, then you will have an opportunity to share your answers with the rest of your group. Finally, we will end with a concluding thought and a time for sharing prayer requests. Your discussion leader may ask for a volunteer to close in prayer. If you are taking this course individually, via the internet, then you can check the answers to your homework on line at www.basicbible101.com.

After we finish a section you will take a quiz over those lessons, and at the end of this class you will be given a final exam. Along the way you will be given review notes and "pop" quizzes to remind you of the main points.

Some Class Rules:

1. You will never be asked to read, pray out loud, answer a question or share anything. You will, however be given an opportunity to do so. Your discussion leader will simply say, "would anyone like to read ..." Remember you will get more out of the class if you participate, and it will keep people from getting bored!

Student Notes:

_____

_____

_____

_____

_____

_____

_____

_____

_____

_____

_____

Men who brought us the Bible:

Moses - Tablets of Stone

Jewish Scribes - Scrolls

Hebrew Scholars - Septuagint

Apostles - Letters

Christian Scribes - Dead Sea Scrolls

Jerome under Pope Damasus - Vulgate

John Wycliff - First English version

Johann Gutenberg - First printing

William Tyndale - Layman's version

Martin Luther - Stood for the right

for everyone to study the Bible

King James I - First official public

version of the Bible

Student Notes:

_____

_____

_____

_____

_____

_____

_____

_____

_____

_____

_____

2. There are NO stupid questions -- ask whatever you like. If your discussion leader doesn't know he or she will find the answer, or you can email me at margie@basicbible101.com. If no one knows then we'll just give the various opinions on the matter.

3. The class closes after the fourth week. The reason for this rule is because we will cover so much of the Bible so quickly that it's too difficult to make up the missed weeks. Fill in the answers to these questions as you listen to the lesson presentation.

What is the Bible?

_____

_____

_____

_____

Who wrote it?

_____

_____

_____

_____

How did the Bible get into this form?

_____

_____

_____

_____

Why are there so many versions?

_____

_____

_____

_____

Why is every sentence numbered?

_____

_____

How can you be sure it's accurate?

_____

_____

What's the best way to study the Bible?

_____

_____

_____

What's the homework for next week?

Matthew 1-3; Luke 1-2.

Be sure to return your class registration form.

New Testament

The Gospels

Matthew Mark Luke John

Acts — History of the Church

Romans 1 Corinthians 2 Corinthians Galatians Ephesians Philippians Colossians 1 Thessalonians 2 Thessalonians 1 Timothy 2 Timothy Titus Philemon — Paul's Letters

Hebrews James 1 Peter 2 Peter 1 John 2 John 3 John Jude — Other Letters

Revelations — Prophecy

Student Notes:

_____

_____

_____

_____

_____

_____

_____

_____

_____

_____

_____

_____

_____

Lesson 2 - The Birth of Jesus

Homework Questions

Read: Luke 1 & 2

1. What was Zechariah's punishment for doubting the angel's words?

_____

_____

2. Why was Mary confused by what the angel told her?

_____

_____

_____

3. How did Elizabeth react when she heard Mary's greeting?

_____

_____

_____

4. Why did Joseph and Mary travel to Bethlehem?

_____

_____

_____

5. How would you have reacted if you'd seen a choir of angels in the sky proclaiming the birth of a savior?

_____

_____

6. Why do you think God would allow his son to be born in a barn?

_____

_____

_____

7. Do you think Mary and Joseph understood who their son was?

_____

_____

_____

8. Who do you think Jesus was?

_____

_____

_____

Student Notes:

_____

_____

_____

_____

_____

_____

_____

_____

_____

_____

_____

Lesson Notes:

List some prophesies that described the coming Messiah:

_____

_____

_____

Why does Luke say that he is writing this book, and to whom is he writing?

_____

_____

_____

Why was King Herod so interested in finding the "newborn king"?

_____

_____

_____

What ever happened to Elizabeth's baby, who was he?

_____

_____

_____

Why doesn't John want to baptize Jesus?

_____

_____

_____

When Mary and Joseph lost Jesus, where did they find him?

_____

_____

_____

Points to remember:
1. Jesus was born to a virgin in a barn and placed in a manger -- a humble beginning for a king.
2. John the Baptist proclaimed Jesus to be the messiah.
3. The birth of Jesus was announced to shepherds, and the star drew the wise men bearing gifts for the new king.

For Next Week: Read Matthew 4, Mark 1-3, Luke 2-5, and John 2-4; or just read Luke 4 & 5.

Student Notes:

_____

_____

_____

_____

_____

_____

_____

_____

_____

_____

_____

Homework Questions

Read: Luke 4

1. With what did Satan tempt Jesus? Did this work?

_____

_____

_____

_____

2. How did Jesus resist the temptation?

_____

_____

_____

_____

3. What do you think would have changed for us if Jesus had listened to Satan?

_____

_____

_____

_____

4. When you are tempted, what helps you resist the temptation?

_____

_____

_____

_____

5. In verses 9-10, what do you notice about Satan's knowledge?

_____

_____

_____

_____

6. Do you think this is the last time Jesus is tempted by Satan?

_____

_____

_____

_____

Student Notes:

_____

_____

_____

_____

_____

_____

_____

_____

_____

_____

Lesson Notes:

How is the temptation of Jesus similar to the temptation of Eve back in Genesis?

_____

_____

_____

What surprises you about the people Jesus chooses to call as disciples?

_____

_____

_____

What is Jesus' first miracle?

_____

_____

When Jesus chooses to spend time with a Samaritan woman, how does she react? How do the disciples react? What about the town's people?

_____

_____

_____

_____

Points to remember:
1. Jesus was an unusual man, able to withstand temptation, do miracles and cross cultural barriers.
2. When Jesus called someone to be his disciple they gave up everything to follow Christ.
3. As word spread about Jesus people came to check him out.
4. Reactions toward Jesus varied greatly.

For Next Week: Read Matthew 5-7, Mark 4, and Luke 6, 8 & 15; or just read Matthew 5 and Luke 15.

Where did Satan come from?

The Bible doesn't tell us much about where Satan came from, but it does give us some clues. 2 Pet. 2:4 mentions that God did not spare the angels when they sinned but cast them into hell. Apparently a rebellion occurred in heaven sometime between Genesis 1:31 and Genesis 3. Among the angels, the heavenly beings that God created to help him in his work, a leader arose who believed he was just as good as God. Isaiah seems to describe this evil one in Isaiah 14:12-15. We commonly call this rebellious head angel Satan. The book of Job gives us more insight into this devilish being in that he comes before God and harasses mankind when God permits it. Satan is referred to as the "father of lies" (John 8:44) and "the evil one" (Matt. 13:19). We know that Satan's power is limited by God. Eventually the Son of God, Jesus Christ, will finish his work on earth and destroy Satan once and for all (Rev. 20:1-3). In the mean time Satan prowls among mankind with the intent on coming between us and God, and eventually destroying us. (2 Pet. 5:8). Our response should be to stay close to God and resist the devil. (For a more in depth discussion see "Satan & Demons," p. 412 in _Systematic Theology_ by Wayne Gruden)

Student Notes:

_____

_____

_____

_____

_____

_____

_____

_____

_____

_____

_____

_____

_____

Homework Questions

Read: Matthew 5 & Luke 15

1. How do you think the crowd felt when they heard Jesus teach?

_____

_____

2. What made his teachings so controversial?

_____

_____

3. Did Jesus do away with the Law that these Jews held sacred?

_____

_____

_____

4. Do you think the crowd understood the parables Jesus taught?

_____

_____

5. In Luke 15 Jesus talks about lost things. What is his point?

_____

_____

6. Do you think the people understood that they were lost?

_____

_____

7. What about the story of the lost son gives you hope?

_____

_____

8. Why did the older brother complain to his father?

_____

_____

9. When you read about the teachings of Jesus how does it effect you personally?

_____

_____

Student Notes:

_____

_____

_____

_____

_____

_____

_____

_____

_____

_____

Basic Bible 101 © 2003 Margaret A. Smith www.basicbible101.com

Lesson Notes:

What is a "parable"?

_____

_____

Who were the Pharisees and why didn't Jesus like them?

_____

_____

When Jesus teaches he expands on the 10 commandments in a new way. Why are his teachings so much more strict?

_____

_____

_____

Is it possible to "Love your enemies"?

_____

_____

List some of your favorite parables here:

_____

_____

_____

_____

_____

_____

Points to remember:
1. Jesus taught with authority, as if God himself was teaching.
2. Jesus taught in parables so that the people could relate to him.
3. Jesus' teachings were controversial and caused many to criticize him and question his credentials to teach.

For Next Week: Read Matthew 8-10, Mark 5-9, and Luke 7, 9-19; and John 5-11; Or just read Mark 6:30-44 "Jesus feeds the 5000" and Matthew 17:1-13 "The Transfiguration of Jesus".

Student Notes:

_____

_____

_____

_____

_____

_____

_____

_____

_____

_____

_____

Lesson 5 - The Miracles

Homework Questions

Read: Mark 6:30-44 and Matthew 17:1-13

1. When Jesus tried to get away for a bit, what did the crowd do?

_____

_____

_____

2. After teaching all day Jesus sees that the crowds are getting hungry. What does he tell his disciples to do?

_____

_____

3. How do they respond?

_____

_____

4. How do you think the disciples felt when they were picking up the left over baskets of food?

_____

_____

5. In Matthew 17, who are the two men that appear with Jesus and why is this significant?

_____

_____

6. How does Peter react to the amazing scene before him?

_____

_____

7. How do you think this experience changed these three disciples' opinion of Jesus?

_____

_____

8. Do you think people would believe in Jesus today if he came and did these miracles in our generation?

_____

_____

9. Would you have believed Jesus was the savior if you'd seen miracles such as these?

_____

_____

Student Notes:

_____

_____

_____

_____

_____

_____

_____

_____

_____

_____

Lesson Notes:

Through his miracles Jesus proves that he is a supernatural man, yet the Pharisees still ask for a sign that he's the messiah. John 7-8 covers the controversy over who people thought Jesus was. List some of their theories here:

_____

_____

_____

_____

When Jesus asks his disciples who they think he is (Luke 9:18-21) what do they say?

_____

_____

List some of the miracles that Jesus did here:

_____

_____

_____

_____

Why did Jesus wait to come to his friend Lazarus?

_____

_____

How did Mary and Martha react to Jesus once he did arrive?

_____

_____

Why did Jesus cry?

_____

_____

Points to remember:
1. Jesus wasn't just a good teacher, he was a miracle worker and master over even death.
2. At the height of his popularity thousands of people followed Jesus, even though they didn't really understand who he was.
3. Jesus feels our hurts just as if they were his own. He was fully man and can relate to all our troubles, but he was also fully God.

For Next Week: For your homework read the accounts of Jesus' trial and crucifixion in Matt. 21-27, Mark 11-15, Luke 19-23 and/or John 12-19; or just do the homework assignment Luke 22:47-62.

Student Notes:

_____

_____

_____

_____

_____

_____

_____

_____

_____

_____

_____

_____

Homework Questions

Read: Luke 22:47-62

1. What did Peter say to the first person who thought they recognized him?

_____

_____

2. What made the people standing around suspect Peter was with Jesus?

_____

_____

3. What did Peter do when he heard the rooster crow?

_____

_____

4. Why did Peter deny he knew Jesus when he had sworn earlier that he would never leave him (v. 33)?

_____

_____

5. When are you tempted to deny Jesus?

_____

_____

6. Where were all the other disciples during this time of confusion?

_____

_____

Student Notes:

_____

_____

_____

_____

_____

_____

_____

_____

_____

_____

_____

_____

7. Do you think it would have been easier for the disciples if they'd stuck together instead of scattering?

_____

_____

8. Does anyone stand up for Jesus?

_____

_____

After Jesus' resurrection he gives Peter a chance to redeem himself. (John 21:15-19) Peter knows he has been forgiven and accepts the new assignment Jesus entrusts to him with much more humility and understanding than he had before Jesus was crucified.

Lesson Notes:

Explain the Passover celebration?

_____

_____

The Last Week:

Monday: Jesus threw the money changers out of the temple area. Did Jesus sin when he got angry at this injustice?

_____

_____

Tuesday: Jesus fields questions from the political leaders of Jerusalem. Did Jesus say we need to pay our taxes?

_____

_____

Thursday: The disciples celebrate the last supper with Jesus. His instructions for "remembering him" are what we currently refer to as communion. Leading his disciples to the garden of Gethsemane, what does Jesus ask his disciples to do? Do they do it?

_____

_____

Friday: At Jesus' trial what is the reaction of Pilate to the claims against Jesus? Of Herod? Who finally pronounces the verdict?

_____

_____

_____

Points to remember:
1. Jesus committed no crime, was guilty of no sin, and gave his life freely even though he could have stopped the whole process at any time.
2. The two main ordinances celebrated today by Christian churches are baptism and communion.
3. The Jews today still celebrate the Passover which commemorates the release of God's people from bondage. Christians know that Jesus was the passover lamb who was slain to buy our freedom from sin and eternal punishment.

For Next Week:
Next week we will see that Jesus reappears, in a new form, and we call that blessed morning Easter! For your homework read the accounts of the resurrection in Matt. 28, Mark 16, Luke 24 and/or John 20-21; or just do the homework assignment in John 20.

Student Notes:

_____

_____

_____

_____

_____

_____

_____

_____

_____

_____

_____

Lesson 7 - The Resurrection

Homework Questions

Read: John 20

1. Mary Magdalene went to Jesus' tomb early Sunday morning, but what did she find?

_____

_____

2. What did Mary think had happened to Jesus' body?

_____

_____

3. When did she realize it was Jesus speaking to her?

_____

_____

4. What did Jesus tell Mary to do?

_____

_____

5. When Jesus appeared to the disciples, did they believe it was really him?

_____

_____

6. What did it take for Thomas to believe it was Jesus speaking to him?

_____

_____

7. In verse 29, who did Jesus say would be blessed?

_____

_____

8. Is it easy for you to believe things without proof?

_____

_____

9. What does it mean to you that Jesus didn't stay dead?

_____

_____

_____

_____

Student Notes:

_____

_____

_____

_____

_____

_____

_____

_____

_____

_____

Basic Bible 101 © 2003 Margaret A. Smith www.basicbible101.com

Lesson Notes:

What strange events happened at Jesus' death?

_____

_____

Describe Jesus' physical appearance after returning from the dead?

_____

_____

When Jesus asked Peter "do you love me" what was his response? How many times did he ask? Why?

_____

_____

_____

_____

What does it mean to mankind that Jesus died, was buried, then rose from the grave?

_____

_____

_____

What "Great Commission" did Jesus give to his followers?

_____

_____

Points to remember:
1. Jesus didn't stay dead. He appeared first to Mary, then two disciples, then more of his disciples, then to Thomas, then to many.
2. Because Jesus died for our sins, and conquered even death we can be confident of forgiveness of sin and eternal life if we believe in him.
3. Jesus' resurrection body was real, touchable and could digest food!
4. Our responsibility as followers of Christ is to "make disciples."

For Next Week:
Next week we will discover what happened with these followers of Jesus. For your homework read the accounts of the early church in Acts 1-12, or just read the homework passage, Acts 2 and 9.

Student Notes:

_____

_____

_____

_____

_____

_____

_____

_____

_____

_____

_____

Homework Questions

Read: Acts 2, 6:8-15 and 7

1. Why do you think some of the locals thought the disciples were drunk?

_____

_____

2. Peter was just a fisherman, how did he get the ability to preach so eloquently?

_____

_____

3. What was the response from the crowd?

_____

_____

4. How did the believers treat one another after this great outpouring of the Holy Spirit?

_____

_____

5. Who stirred up the trouble against Stephen and why?

_____

_____

Student Notes:

_____

_____

_____

_____

_____

_____

_____

_____

_____

_____

6. What did Stephen say that angered the Sanhedrin so much that they wanted to kill him?

_____

_____

7. How could Stephen be so forgiving when he was dying by the hand of sinful men?

_____

_____

8. Who stood watching this scene and holding everyone's coats (8:1)?

_____

_____

Lesson Notes:

What physical sign did the believers see when the Spirit descended on them?

_____

_____

What were the believers able to do as a result of this indwelling of the Holy Spirit?

_____

_____

In what tangible ways did the believers show the love of Christ to the outside world?

_____

_____

How did Peter respond to the beggar outside the temple?

_____

_____

The political leaders of Jerusalem probably thought they'd ended the uprising over Jesus of Nazareth when they crucified him. When Peter and John continue to preach Jesus they are thrown in prison. What happens to them in prison? What do they do as soon as they are released?

_____

_____

_____

Points to remember:
1. The Holy Spirit is real and can change your life.
2. Believers become family, that's why we refer to each other as "brothers and sisters in Christ."
3. You may be asked to suffer for your faith.
4. The believers scattered because of the persecution of their faith, thus the gospel spread throughout Judea and Samaria.

For Next Week:
We will be introduced to Saul and the impact he will have on the early church. Read Acts 8-20, or just Acts 8-9 for the homework.

Student Notes:

_____

_____

_____

_____

_____

_____

_____

_____

_____

_____

_____

Homework Questions

Read: Acts 9

1. Who was Saul and on who's authority was he capturing Christians?

_____

_____

2. What happens to him on the road to Damascus?

_____

_____

3. Why was Ananias hesitant to believe Saul's story?

_____

_____

4. What does Ananias do for Saul?

_____

_____

5. When Saul starts preaching to the Jews in Damascus how do they respond?

_____

_____

6. Who sponsors Saul in Jerusalem?

_____

_____

7. Have you ever had someone stand up for you when you were the outsider? How did it make you feel?

_____

_____

8. It took a major event to get Saul's attention and change his attitude toward Jesus. What did it take, or would it take, to change your attitude toward Jesus?

_____

_____

_____

Student Notes:

_____

_____

_____

_____

_____

_____

_____

_____

_____

_____

Basic Bible 101 © 2003 Margaret A. Smith www.basicbible101.com

Lesson Notes

Why did Saul think he was justified in persecuting Christians?

_____

_____

What insight does the Lord give Ananias into who Saul would become?

_____

_____

What was Peter's vision and why was it so disturbing for him?

_____

_____

What is the response in Cornelius' household when Peter preached to them?

_____

Why did Peter have some trouble with the believers back in Jerusalem? What were their attitudes toward Gentiles?

_____

_____

Points to remember:
1. When God gets hold of you he changes you to the very core of your being.
2. Take a risk and stand up for someone when you sense they may be telling the truth.
3. Old traditions must die if you're going to be free to serve God – he makes the rules.
4. Crossing cultural norms to share the story of Jesus is part of accomplishing the great commission.

For Next Week:
For next week read through the journeys of Paul, Acts 13 – 28. Along the way Paul writes to many of the people he met, and those letters become the books of Romans, Galatians, Ephesians, and so on. We'll work on our maps next week as well.

Student Notes:

_____

_____

_____

_____

_____

_____

_____

_____

_____

_____

_____

Homework Questions

Read: Acts 13-15

In the maps on the following pages find the one labeled "Paul's First Journey." As you read through Acts 13 trace the route Paul took.

1. List some of the hardships Paul faced:

_____

_____

_____

_____

2. What problems did he face with the church in Jerusalem?

_____

_____

3. What argument did he give for why Gentiles should be considered Christians without making them follow Jewish laws?

_____

_____

4. After making this argument with the church in Jerusalem he wrote back to the Galatians. Read this book and comment on it's content:

_____

_____

5. Why did Paul object to taking John Mark along with them for the second journey? Trace this route as you read about his second trip.

_____

_____

6. This disagreement spawned two missionary teams. In your life, when has a disagreement with another ended with positive results?

_____

_____

_____

During his second journey Paul wrote to the Thessalonians from Corinth. Read these books in your Bible and write a few words to describe the theme of the books:

_____

_____

Student Notes:

_____

_____

_____

_____

_____

_____

_____

_____

_____

_____

Lesson Notes

Paul is discipled by Barnabus for an entire year in Antioch. The two feel called to travel through Cyprus and into Lycaonia (modern day Turkey). As a result of their journey many believed and several new churches began. On his second journey he headed for Asia but turned back to Macedonia. Why?

_____

_____

On his second journey Paul and Silas are thrown into prison. What made the crowd so mad?

_____

_____

When an opportunity to escape prison arises Paul and Silas remain in the prison. What does the jailer do when he finds them still in their cell?

_____

_____

When in Athens Paul sees lots of idols, but specifically he sees one to "the unknown God". How does Paul use this idol to reason with the people there?

_____

_____

Completing his third missionary journey, Paul stops near Ephesus and asks the elders of the Ephesus church to come see him. What does the prophet there tell Paul? How does Paul react?

_____

_____

Back in Jerusalem Paul is about to be killed but he appeals to Caesar. His fourth journey, the journey to Rome, has some exciting moments. What are they?

_____

_____

Points to remember:
The early church owes much of its growth to Paul and other missionaries like him, who boldly preached despite great persecution and at a tremendous personal cost. Christianity is costly.

For Next Week:
Next week we will cover the letters of Paul. Read as many as you can: Romans, 1 & 2 Corinthians, Galatians, Ephesians, Philippians Colossians, 1 & 2 Thessalonians, 1 & 2 Timothy, Titus, Philemon.

Student Notes:

_____

_____

_____

_____

_____

_____

_____

_____

_____

_____

_____

Paul's First Missionary Journey

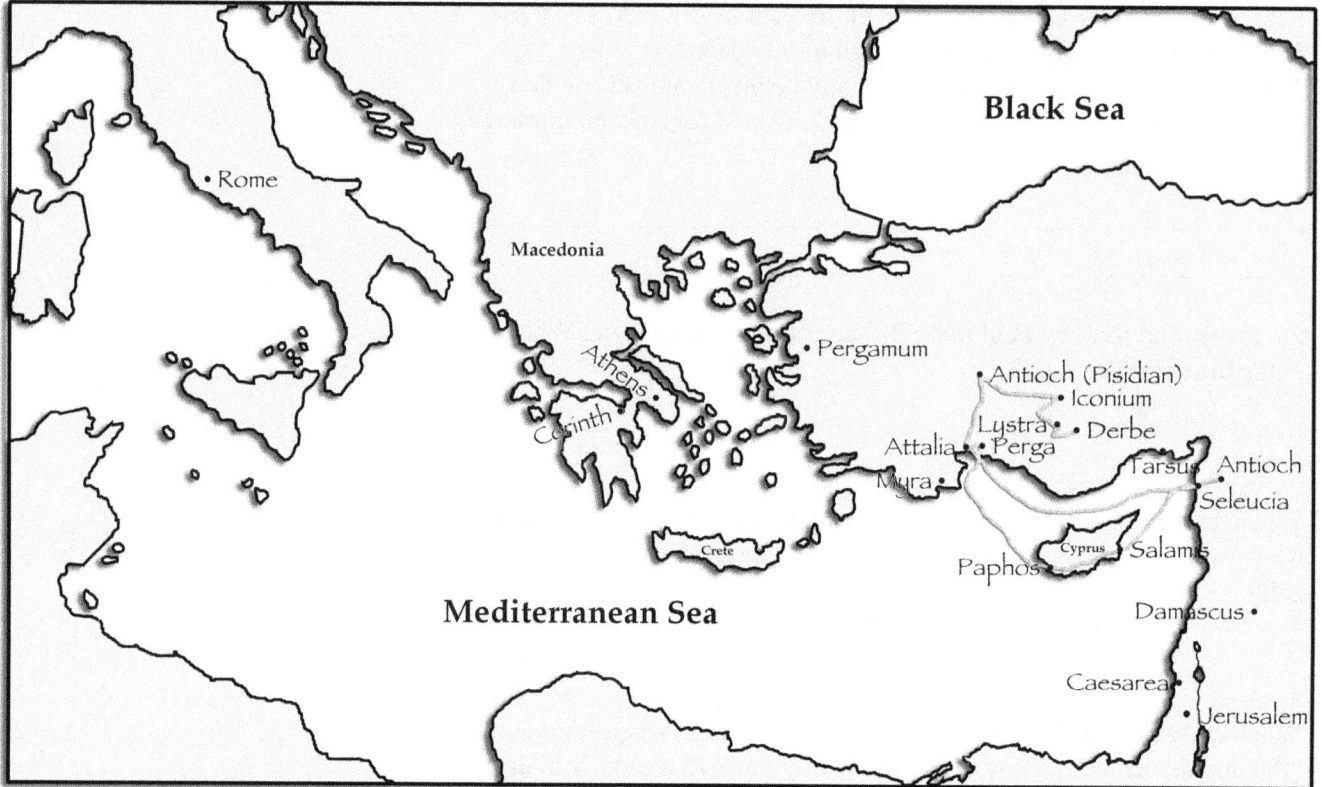

Paul's Second Missionary Journey

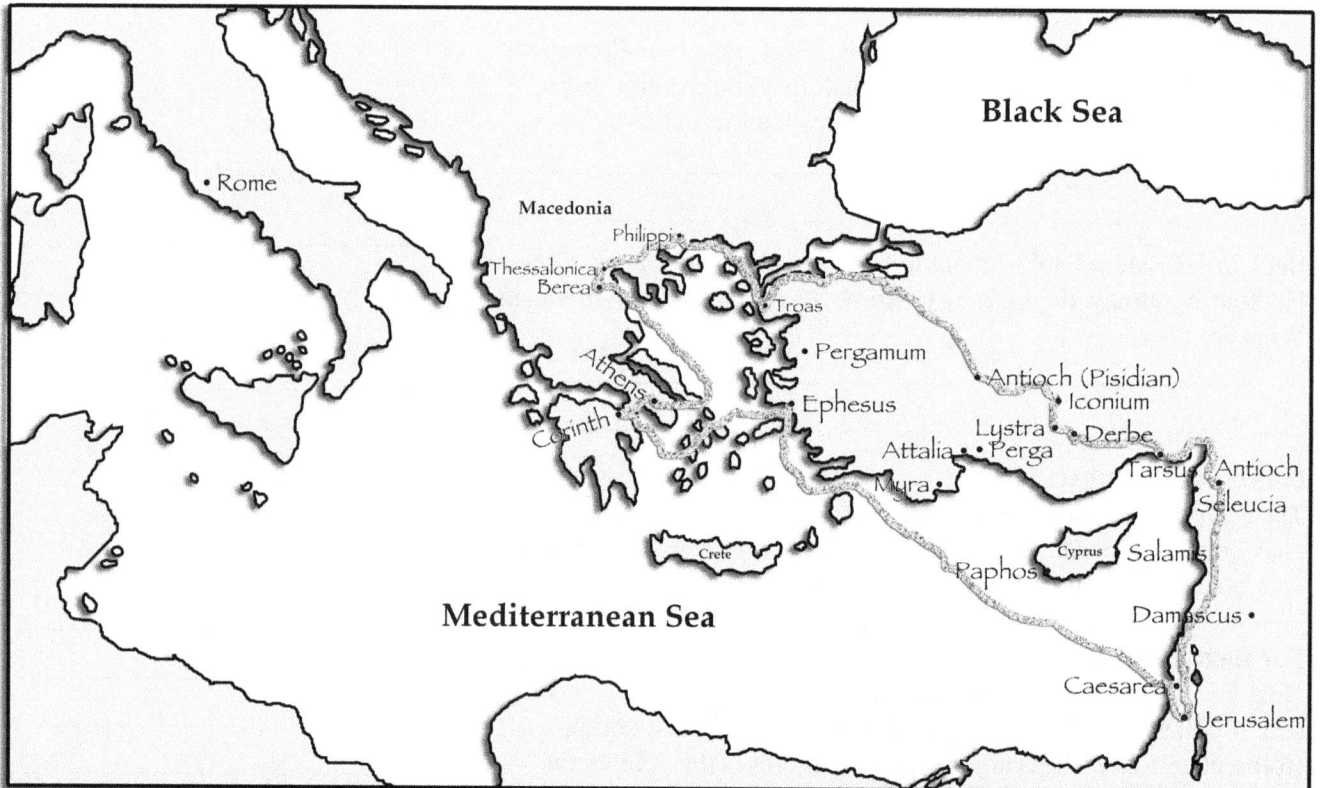

Paul's Third Missionary Journey

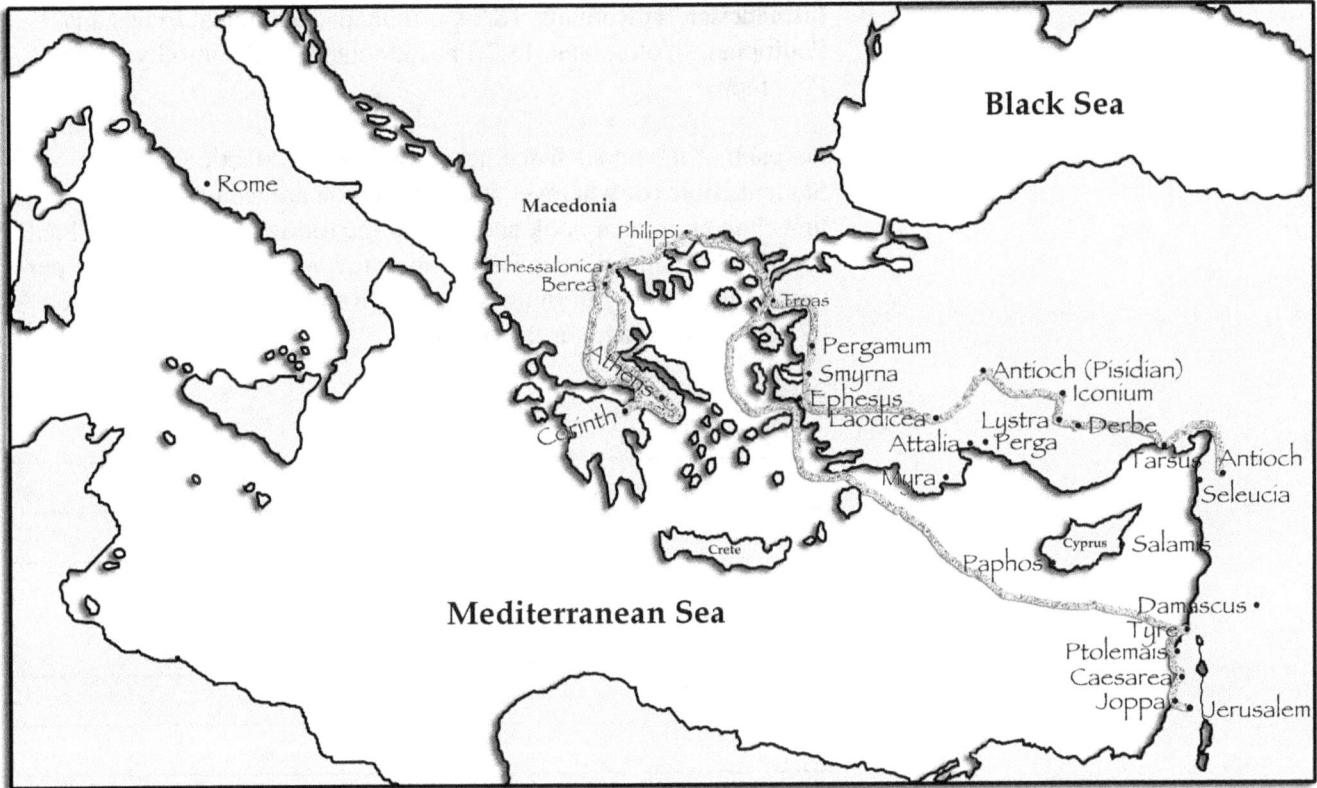

Black Sea

Rome

Macedonia

Philippi

Thessalonica
Berea

Troas

Pergamum

Smyrna
Ephesus
Laodicea

Antioch (Pisidian)

Iconium

Lystra
Perga

Derbe

Athens

Attalia

Corinth

Mura

Tarsus

Antioch

Seleucia

Cyprus

Salamis

Crete

Paphos

Damascus

Tyre

Ptolemais

Caesarea

Joppa

Jerusalem

Mediterranean Sea

Paul's Journey to Rome

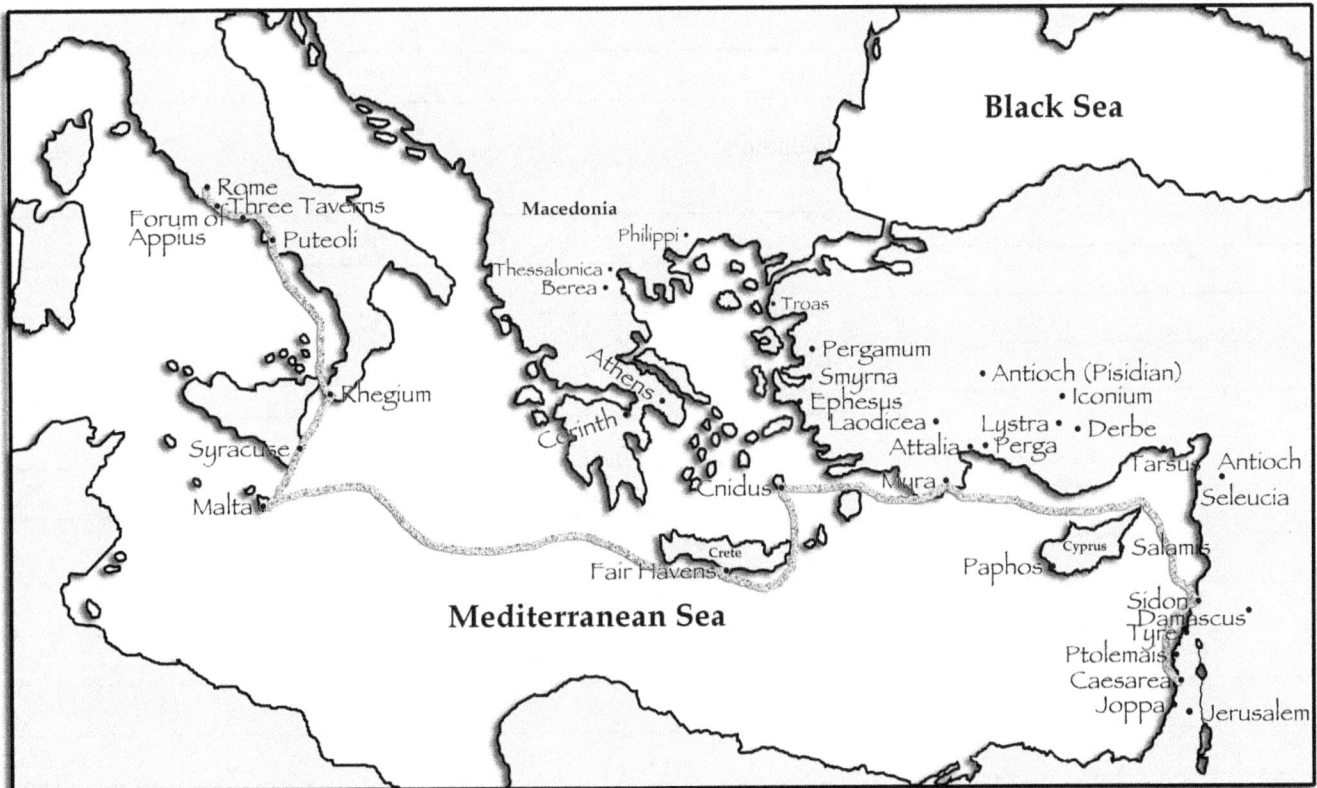

Black Sea

Rome
Three Taverns

Forum of
Appius

Puteoli

Macedonia

Philippi

Thessalonica
Berea

Troas

Rhegium

Athens

Pergamum

Smyrna
Ephesus
Laodicea

Antioch (Pisidian)

Iconium

Lystra
Perga

Derbe

Syracuse

Corinth

Attalia

Malta

Cnidus

Mura

Tarsus

Antioch

Seleucia

Crete

Cyprus

Salamis

Fair Havens

Paphos

Sidon
Damascus
Tyre

Ptolemais

Caesarea

Joppa

Jerusalem

Mediterranean Sea

Homework Questions

Introduction to: Romans, 1&2 Corinthians, Galatians, Ephesians, Philippians, Colossians, 1&2 Thessalonians, 1&2 Timothy, Titus, Philemon

For each of the books listed here, read the introduction in your Student Bible (or whatever study Bible you are using). Then read the first chapter of each book and answer the following: How does Paul describe himself? Who is Paul writing to? What seems to be the purpose of the letter? Fill in missing info from the lesson as presented by your group leader or the podcast.

Romans:

_____

_____

_____

1 Corinthians:

_____

_____

_____

2 Corinthians:

_____

_____

_____

Galatians:

_____

_____

_____

Ephesians:

_____

_____

_____

Philippians:

_____

_____

Student Notes:

_____

_____

_____

_____

_____

_____

_____

_____

_____

_____

_____

Basic Bible 101 © 2003 Margaret A. Smith www.basicbible101.com

Colossians:

_____

_____

_____

1 Thessalonians:

_____

_____

_____

2 Thessalonians:

_____

_____

_____

1 Timothy:

_____

_____

_____

2 Timothy:

_____

_____

_____

Titus:

_____

_____

_____

Philemon:

_____

_____

_____

Points to remember:

Much of the doctrine Christians hold true was developed by Paul. In his letters he connects the Old Testament prophecies and Jewish teachings with the messiah Jesus Christ. His letters are personal, yet offered practical solutions to guide the early church.

For Next Week:

Read as many as you can of Hebrews, James, 1 & 2 Peter, 1, 2 & 3 John, and Jude.

Student Notes:

_____

_____

_____

_____

_____

_____

_____

_____

_____

_____

_____

_____

_____

Lesson 12 - The Other Letters

Homework Questions

Introduction to: Hebrews, James, 1 & 2 Peter, 1, 2 & 3 John, and Jude.

For each of the books listed here, read the introduction in your Student Bible (or whatever study Bible you are using). Then read the first chapter of each book and answer the following: How does the author describe himself? Who is the author writing to? What seems to be the purpose of the letter? Fill in missing info from the lesson as presented by your group leader or the podcast.

Hebrews:

_____

_____

_____

James:

_____

_____

_____

1 Peter:

_____

_____

_____

2 Peter:

_____

_____

_____

1 John:

_____

_____

_____

2 John:

_____

_____

_____

Student Notes:

_____

_____

_____

_____

_____

_____

_____

_____

_____

_____

_____

3 John:

_____

_____

_____

Jude:

_____

_____

_____

How do these letters differ from the ones Paul wrote?

_____

_____

What common themes are repeated throughout the letters in the New
Testament?

_____

_____

_____

_____

Which of these letters (or Paul's letters) is your favorite and why?

_____

_____

_____

Points to remember:
*The early churches were far apart and it was difficult to
communicate with one another. Usually one letter would be carried
to many different cities and read to the church at that city. These
letters helped the early believers to share burdens, learn from one
another and receive encouragement as the persecution of Christians
became more commonplace.*

For Next Week:
Read as much of Revelations as you can, or just read the first three
chapters for the homework questions.

Student Notes:

_____

_____

_____

_____

_____

_____

_____

_____

_____

_____

_____

Lesson 13 - Revelations

Homework Questions

Read: Revelations 1-3

1. Who is writing this narrative?

_____

2. Who is he writing to?

_____

3. What words of praise and warning does he have for each church? To the church in Ephesus:

_____

_____

To the church in Smyrna:

_____

_____

To the church in Pergamum:

_____

_____

To the church in Thyatria:

_____

_____

To the church in Sardis:

_____

_____

To the church in Philadelphia:

_____

_____

To the church in Laodicea:

_____

_____

Which of these churches is most like your church and why?

_____

_____

What promises are given for the churches that overcome?

_____

_____

Student Notes:

_____

_____

_____

_____

_____

_____

_____

_____

_____

_____

Lesson Notes

Who is worthy to open the scroll (5:2)?

_____

What prophesies are revealed with the breaking of each seal?

_____

_____

_____

_____

_____

_____

_____

In chapter 7 verses 9-17 who are these people who escape the great tribulation?

_____

_____

After all the fighting and tribulation, who is victorious?

_____

In the last chapter of Revelations, what are the consequences for anyone who adds to or subtracts from this revelation?

_____

_____

When will Jesus return to the earth?

_____

_____

Points to remember:
Many people have attempted to interpret Revelations, but no one knows for sure what all the images in this book mean. Some may have already occurred, others may be yet to come. Don't get sidetracked by the details in prophecy, rather focus on the overall message and what it means for us today.

For Next Week:
Prepare for the final exam by studying the New Testament Review available online and in the Leader's Guide.

Student Notes:

_____

_____

_____

_____

_____

_____

_____

_____

_____

_____

_____

About the Author

Raised in a relatively conservative Christian home, Margie Smith found the truths of Christ easy to accept. As a youth she personalized these truths and was baptized, joining a Southern Baptist Church in Spokane, Washington. In college she and her husband Brian attended a rather unconventional Free Evangelical church, attending a weekly couples Bible study and working in the Baptist Student Ministries on campus.

In 1987 Margie and Brian moved to Dallas, Texas with their two children. Margie has been a life-long student of the Bible, teaching various childrens and adult Bible classes along the way. She has served as both a Small Group Leader and Coach.

Margie is currently a member of Woodcreek Church, Richardson, Texas. Additionally, she owns a Dallas-based advertising agency.

She has always enjoyed working with new believers. Margie developed the Basic Bible 101 curriculum as a way to bridge the gap when adults become believers in Christ and attempt to understand the Bible for the first time in their lives.

Answers to the Homework and Lesson Notes
Answers to the questions posed in the homework and lesson notes can be found online at http://www.basicbible101.com under the Lesson Notes heading.

Quizzes, Handouts, Review Sheets and The Final Exam
To access the quizzes, handouts, review sheets and the final exam, log into the student area of the website using **student** as the username and **basicbible101** as the password.

How to Order More Workbooks
Basic Bible 101 New Testament Student Workbooks and Leader's Guide can be purchased online through the Basic Bible 101 website (http://www.basicbible101.com) or you can write to:

Basic Bible 101
c/o Margie Smith
PO Box 941843
Plano, TX 75094

Email: margie@basicbible101.com

An Old Testament version of this course is also available.

www.ingramcontent.com/pod-product-compliance
Lightning Source LLC
LaVergne TN
LVHW061342060426
835511LV00014B/2064